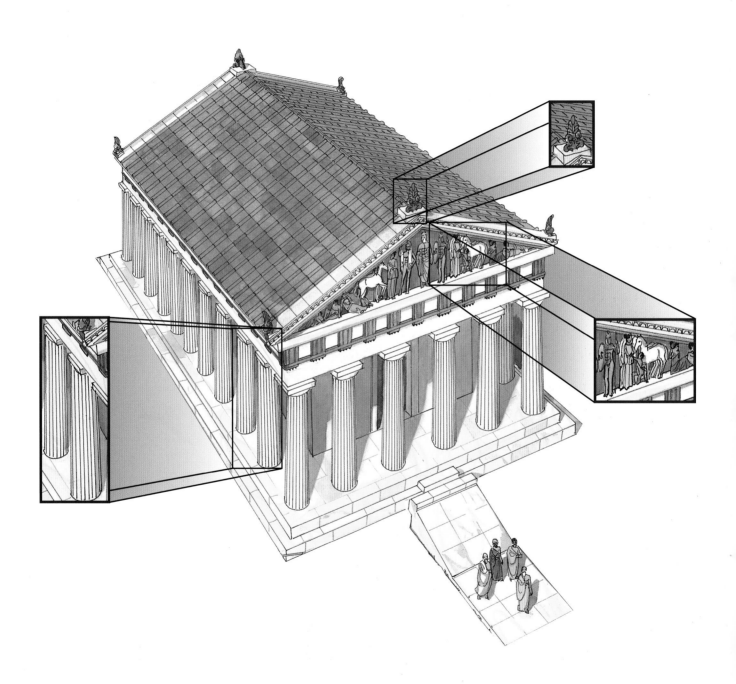

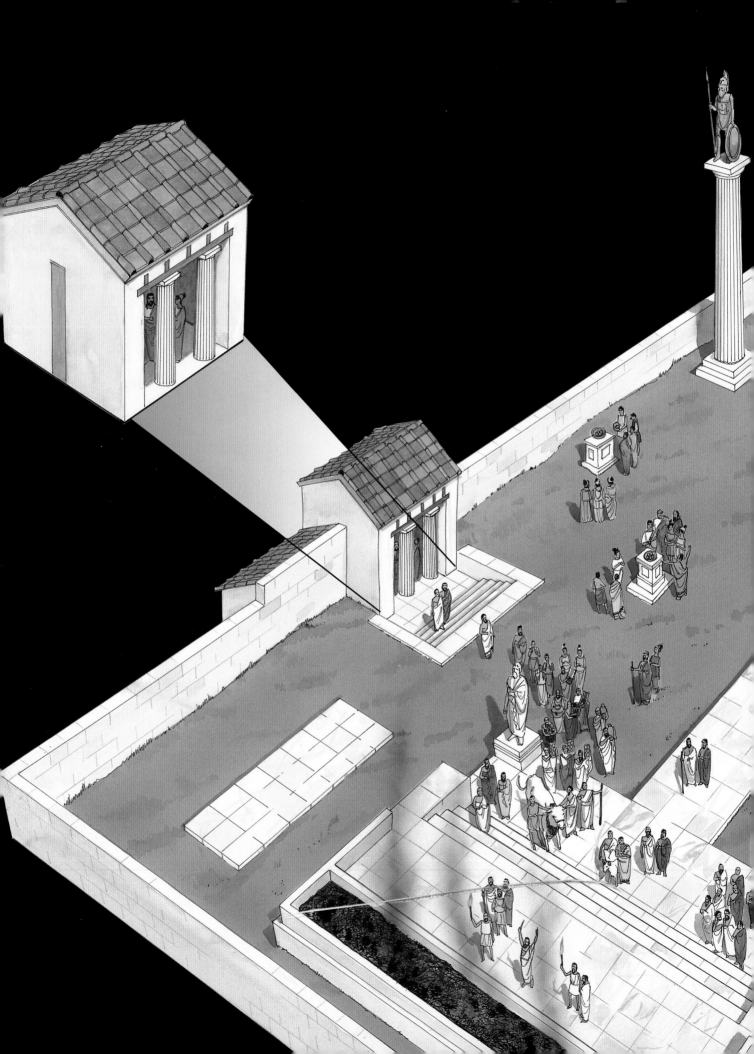

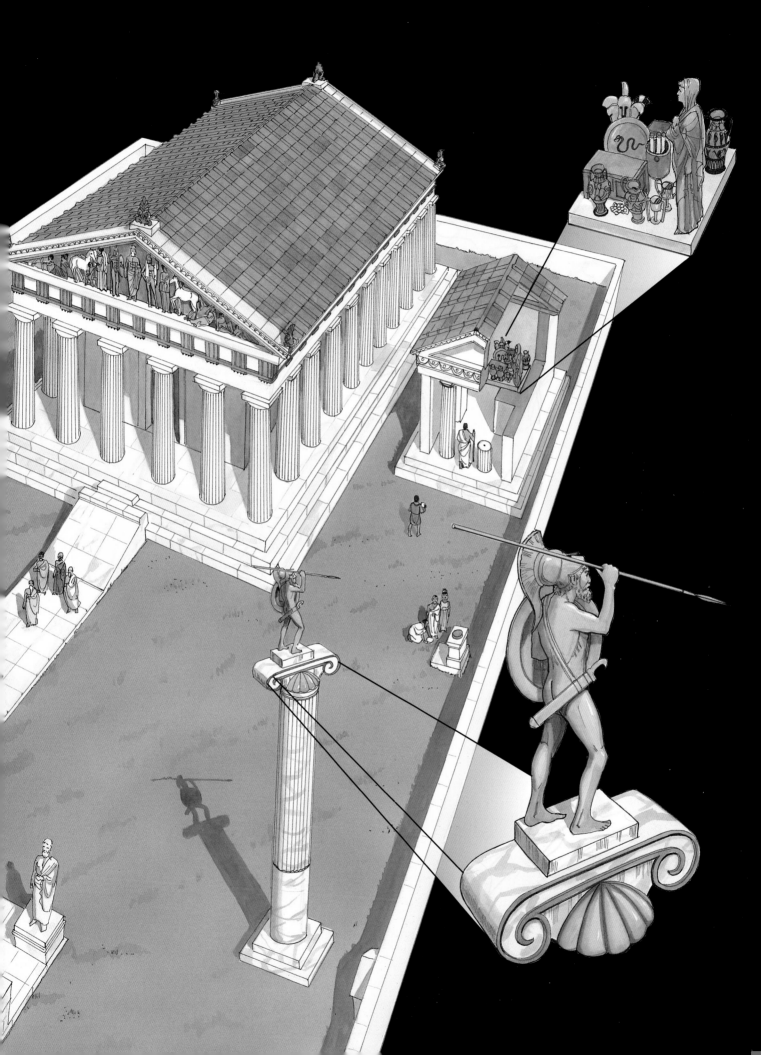

Author:

John Malam studied Ancient History and Archaeology at the University of Birmingham, after which he worked as an archaeologist at the Ironbridge Gorge Museum, Shropshire. He is now an author, specializing in information books for children. He lives in Cheshire with his wife, a book designer, and their two children.

Artist:

Mark Bergin was born in Hastings, England, in 1961. He studied at Eastbourne College of Art and has specialized in historical reconstructions, aviation, and maritime subjects since 1983. He has illustrated **A Roman Fort** in the *Pinpoints* series. He lives in Bexhill-on-Sea with his wife and three children.

Series creator:

David Salariya was born in Dundee, Scotland. In 1989 he established The Salariya Book Company. He has designed and created many new series for publishers in the UK and overseas. He lives in Brighton with his wife, the illustrator Shirley Willis, and their son Jonathan.

Editor:

Karen Barker Smith

Assistant Editor:

Stephanie Cole

First published in hardback in Great Britain in MMIII by
Book House, an imprint of
The Salariya Book Company Ltd
25 Marlborough Place, Brighton BN1 1UB

SALARIYA
Visit
www.salariya.com
for our online catalogue and
free fun stuff.

ISBN: 978-1-905638-62-8

A CIP catalogue record for this book is available from the British Library.

Printed and bound in China.
Printed on paper from sustainable forests.
Reprinted in MMXVIII.

CONTENTS

AN ANCIENT GREEK TEMPLE

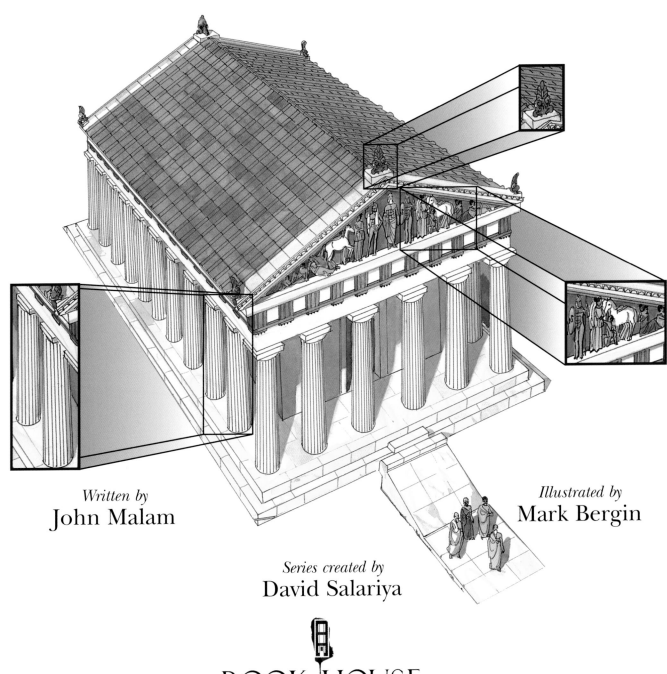

Written by
John Malam

Illustrated by
Mark Bergin

Series created by
David Salariya

BOOK HOUSE
a SALARIYA imprint

An actor with a mask

Epidauros was important for two reasons. It was a centre of healing, where the sick went to be cured, and it was home to a huge open-air theatre. As many as 12,000 spectators at a time watched actors perform plays there.

Oracle priestess at Delphi

Delphi was a place of pilgrimage for people from all over the Greek world. Here they believed they could talk to the god Apollo through an oracle priestess, who was the god's messenger on Earth.

Mount Olympus, the highest mountain in Greece, was believed to be the home of the twelve most important Greek gods, the Olympians.

Zeus, the weather god and father of the gods

Olympia was a vast sports complex. It was here that the Olympic Games were held every four years. Athletes came from all parts of the Greek world to compete in the festival of sport, which lasted for five days.

Athlete throwing a discus

In a Minoan ceremony, men and women leapt over a bull

Crete was the home of the Minoan civilization between c.3200 BC to 1100 BC. Even though the Minoans lived and died before the rise of the ancient Greeks, the Greeks knew about them and told stories about them. Knossos was a Minoan town.

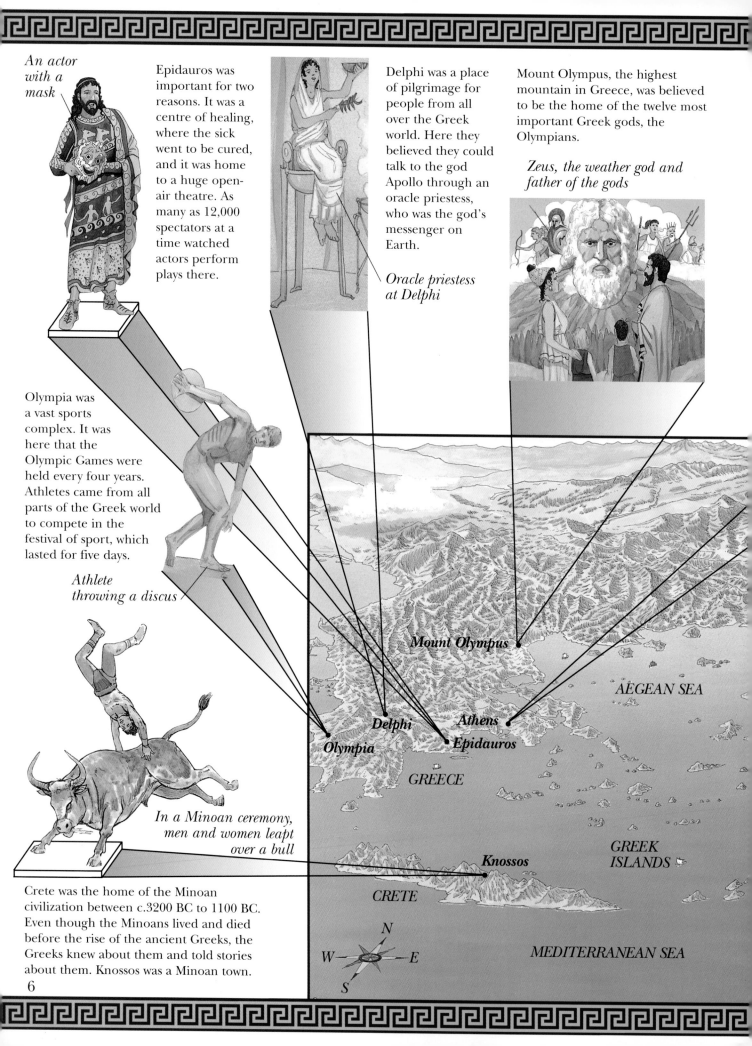

Mount Olympus

AEGEAN SEA

Delphi

Athens

Epidauros

Olympia

GREECE

Knossos

GREEK ISLANDS

CRETE

N
W   E
S

MEDITERRANEAN SEA

The Parthenon temple at Athens was dedicated to the goddess Athena Parthenos, whose gold and ivory statue stood inside.

ANCIENT GREECE

ABOUT 2,500 YEARS AGO, the people of Greece became the first great civilization in mainland Europe. On the fertile plains of the peninsula and on the many islands scattered throughout the warm, blue water of the Aegean Sea, Greek society blossomed. It was at its finest between about 500 and 300 BC – the 'golden age' of the ancient Greek people. They made great progress in the sciences, the arts, sport and politics. Some Greek towns became famous for particular reasons and are pinpointed on the map, below. Athens emerged as the most important city and it was here that the finest of all Greek temples was built, the Parthenon. However, every town had a temple and this book shows how these buildings were planned, erected and used by the ancient Greeks.

Ancient Greek men had more rights than women. They could vote in elections and were considered to be the heads of their families. Women were expected to care for the home and bring children into the world.

Merchant ship

Greek warship

The sea was very important to the Greeks. Socrates, the famous Greek philosopher, said, "We live around a sea like frogs around a pond." He meant that the Greek people were as comfortable on the sea, trading using their merchant ships or fighting in their warships, as they were on land.

A TOWN AND ACROPOLIS

GREEK TOWNS were often built close to a hill or an area of high ground because, in early Greek society, hilltops were used as citadels. Surrounded by strong walls, they were places of refuge and could be easily defended. The hill was called an acropolis, meaning upper city. When no longer needed for defence, the acropolis developed a new use. It became a religious centre, where temples were built and people went to offer prayers and sacrifices to the gods. The hill and its religious buildings became the spiritual heart of each town.

Greek temples grew from simple beginnings. They developed slowly, over many years, until eventually the original old wooden temples were replaced with ones of stone.

Original wooden temple

The town's first temple would have been this small wooden structure (above). In the 5th century BC a grander one of stone would have been built in its place.

Acropolis

Thatched roof

Sports stadium

Ancient pottery models show us what the first Greek temples probably looked like. This model (above), from Perachora, near Corinth, shows a small, one-roomed, wooden temple.

DEVELOPMENT OF TEMPLE ARCHITECTURE

Caves and springs were sacred places to the early Greeks and were believed to be the home of spirits. Shrines were built in these places, where people could pray.

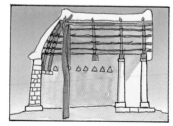

By the 8th century BC, small house-like temples had replaced the shrines. They were meant as homes for the spirits. These first temples were made of timber, as the above cutaway shows.

Gradually, a distinctive style of temple architecture emerged. Stout timbers supported the roof, which in early temples was flat. Temples were still small buildings.

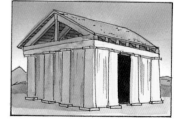

Later, temple roofs were raised up, making a slope down from a central ridge. Still built mainly from timber, temples were now impressive buildings.

8

At the town centre was a large open area, or agora. It was where traders sold their goods from market stalls and where public meetings were held.

Agora

Bouleuterion

Men aged over 18 could vote at the gathering of the town's citizens, known as the Assembly.

Inside the council building, or *bouleterion*, the town's elected councillors held their meetings. It was these officials who decided if a town should have a new temple.

Men aged over 30 could become councillors, the officials who decided how the town should be run.

Harbour

Male citizens voted to decide whether unpopular politicians should be banished from the town, called ostracism.

Sometimes runners raced wearing armour and carrying shields.

Women and foreigners were not allowed to have a say in the political life of a town.

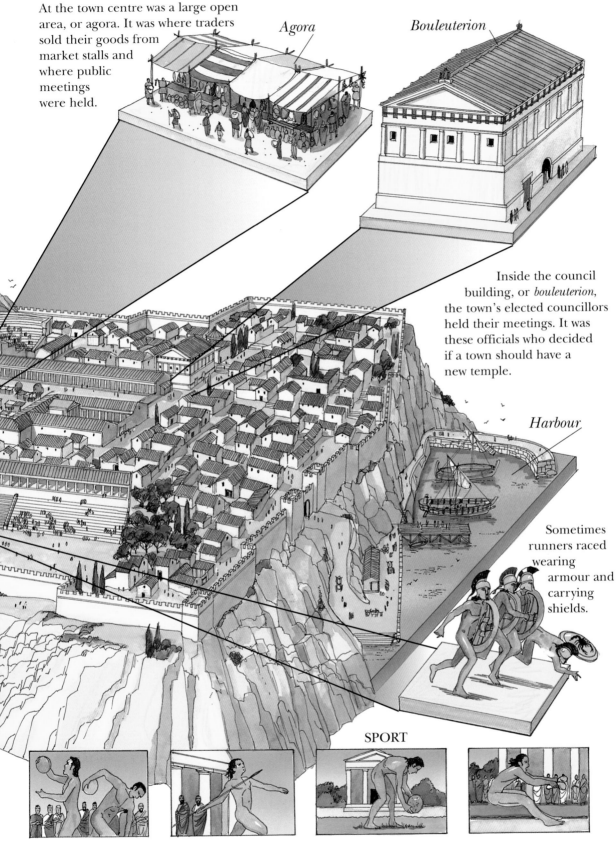

SPORT

Discus-throwing. Made from bronze, lead or stone and weighing about 2.5 kg, a discus could be thrown for up to 30 m.

Javelin-throwing. A thrower used a leather thong to launch his elderwood javelin, which could fly as far as 100 m.

Stone-throwing. In some places, contests were held to see how far heavy stones could be thrown.

Long-jump. Swinging a pair of weights to help them go further, athletes jumped from a standing start.

AT THE QUARRY

LIMESTONE WAS THE MAIN type of stone used by the ancient Greeks for buildings and statues. Called *poros*, it was relatively soft and easy to cut and shape. They also used marble, or *marmaros*. Harder and finer than limestone, marble became the main material used for temples and other important structures. To meet the demand for stone, huge quarries were developed where slaves, criminals and prisoners-of-war were sent to work. It was hard, dangerous work. Because it was difficult and expensive to transport stone, quarries were usually located near to where building was taking place.

QUARRYING A BLOCK OF STONE

A flat area of rock was chosen. Then, a deep groove was chiselled into it, outlining a rectangular block of stone.

Wooden wedges were knocked into the groove. As they entered the rock, they forced it to split a little along the cut.

Hammering wooden wedges into a groove to split rock

When all the wedges were in place, water was poured over them. It ran into the groove and the wooden wedges soaked it up.

The wedges expanded when soaked with water. As they swelled, the rock was forced to split more along the groove.

As the split grew wider and deeper, quarry workers put wooden levers into it. They pulled on them until the block broke away from the rock.

The block was roughly shaped. Excess stone was knocked off, leaving the block slightly bigger than the finished stone needed to be.

Lifting 'handles', called bosses, were left on the sides. The block's final shape and size would be decided at the building site.

Quarries were dangerous places. Most quarries were open-cast, where stone was worked in the open air. But some were like mines, where stone was removed from deep underground. Whatever the type of quarry, there was always the danger of falling rock and many quarry workers died from accidents and exhaustion.

Before a block left the quarry, stonemasons removed excess stone from it (below). This made it lighter and easier to move. They roughly trimmed it into the shape that was needed but left a thin 'jacket' of surplus stone all around it. This protected the stone from damage during transport to the building site.

Roughly trimming a block

Workers could be crushed by falling rock

Rough hewn blocks of stone

Men worked in gangs

Wire

Quarries such as this produced huge quantities of stone. The quarry at Syracuse, a Greek town in Sicily, produced more than 112 million tonnes of limestone during the course of its life.

Sand

To produce thin slabs rather than large blocks, some stone was simply split into thinner pieces. If this wasn't possible, the stone was cut using wire and sand. A groove was scored in the block and filled with sand. Wire was then pulled to and fro along the groove (above), pressing down on the sand – the sand did the cutting, not the wire. As the groove became deeper, more sand was added. Slowly, the sand wore its way right through the stone.

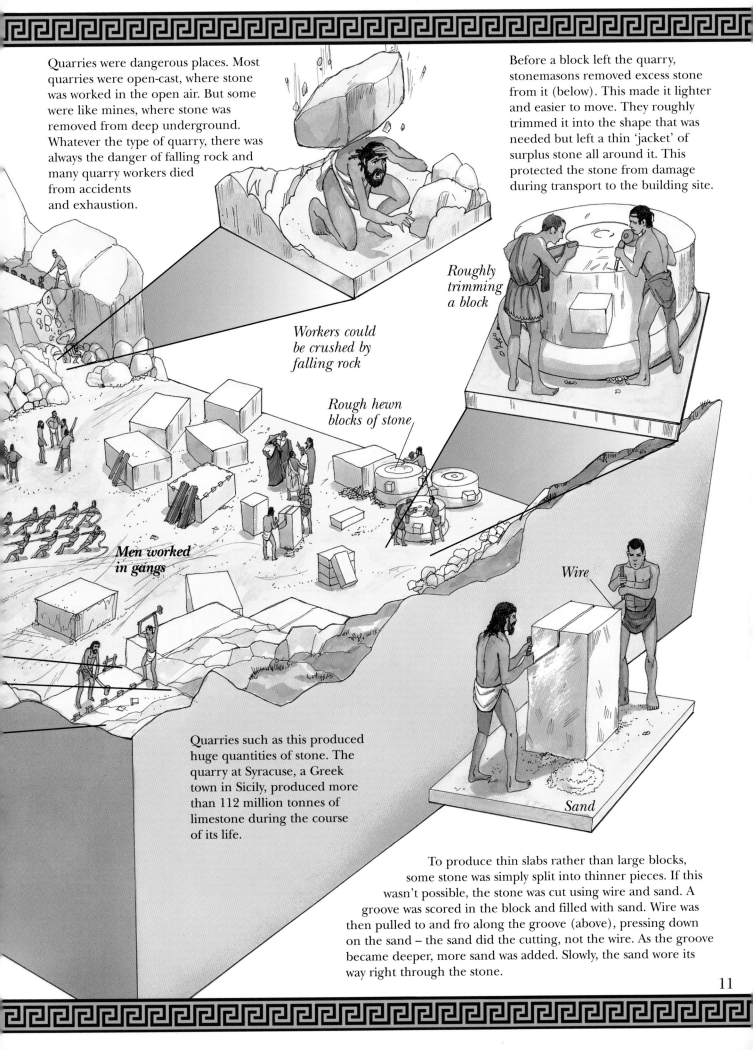

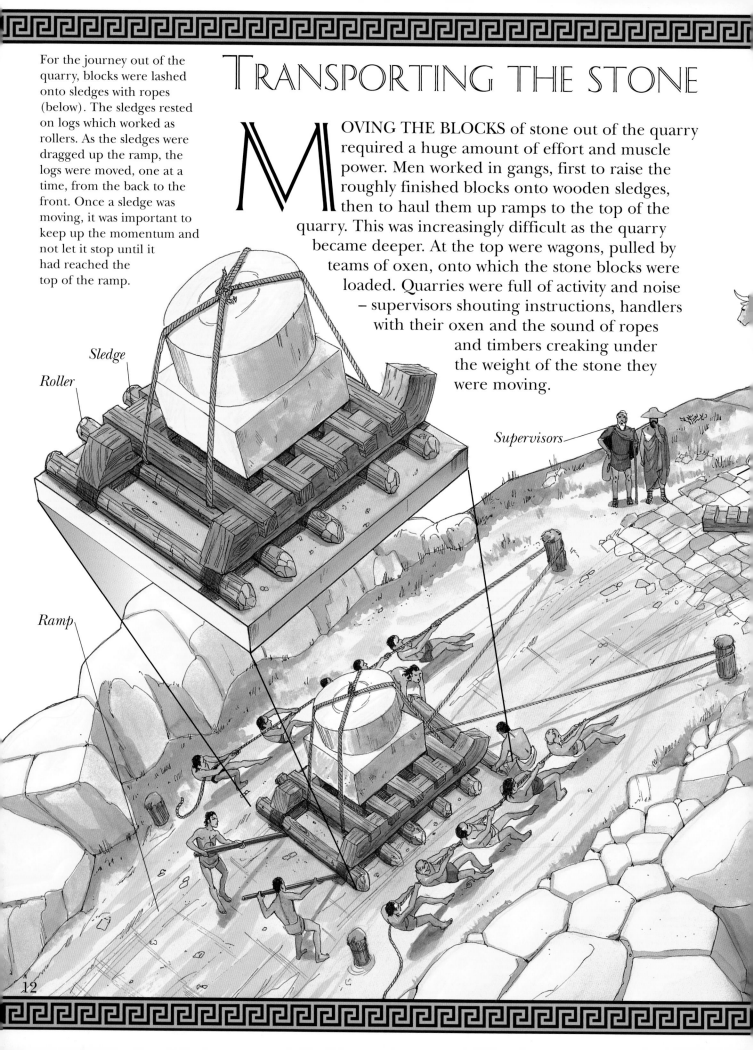

For the journey out of the quarry, blocks were lashed onto sledges with ropes (below). The sledges rested on logs which worked as rollers. As the sledges were dragged up the ramp, the logs were moved, one at a time, from the back to the front. Once a sledge was moving, it was important to keep up the momentum and not let it stop until it had reached the top of the ramp.

MOVING THE BLOCKS of stone out of the quarry required a huge amount of effort and muscle power. Men worked in gangs, first to raise the roughly finished blocks onto wooden sledges, then to haul them up ramps to the top of the quarry. This was increasingly difficult as the quarry became deeper. At the top were wagons, pulled by teams of oxen, onto which the stone blocks were loaded. Quarries were full of activity and noise – supervisors shouting instructions, handlers with their oxen and the sound of ropes and timbers creaking under the weight of the stone they were moving.

Sledge

Roller

Supervisors

Ramp

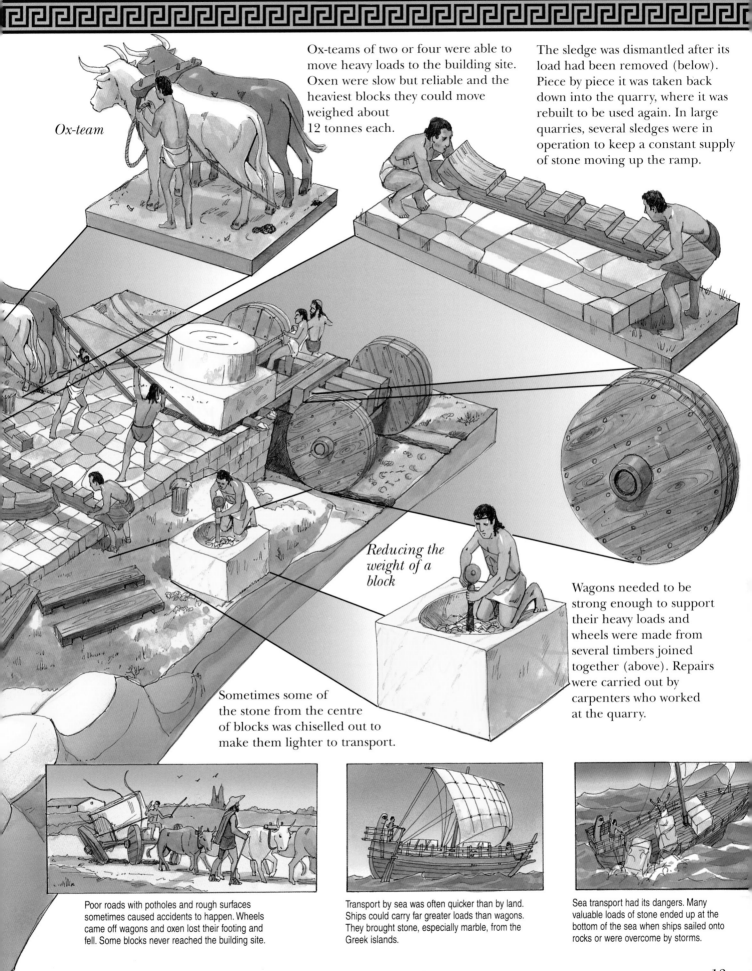

Ox-team

Ox-teams of two or four were able to move heavy loads to the building site. Oxen were slow but reliable and the heaviest blocks they could move weighed about 12 tonnes each.

The sledge was dismantled after its load had been removed (below). Piece by piece it was taken back down into the quarry, where it was rebuilt to be used again. In large quarries, several sledges were in operation to keep a constant supply of stone moving up the ramp.

Reducing the weight of a block

Wagons needed to be strong enough to support their heavy loads and wheels were made from several timbers joined together (above). Repairs were carried out by carpenters who worked at the quarry.

Sometimes some of the stone from the centre of blocks was chiselled out to make them lighter to transport.

Poor roads with potholes and rough surfaces sometimes caused accidents to happen. Wheels came off wagons and oxen lost their footing and fell. Some blocks never reached the building site.

Transport by sea was often quicker than by land. Ships could carry far greater loads than wagons. They brought stone, especially marble, from the Greek islands.

Sea transport had its dangers. Many valuable loads of stone ended up at the bottom of the sea when ships sailed onto rocks or were overcome by storms.

THE BUILDING SITE

A NEW TEMPLE was put together like a giant construction kit. Stone blocks arriving from the quarry were unloaded near the part of the building they were needed for. Before blocks could be put in place, foundations strong enough to support the weight of the temple above them had to be laid. Then, block by block, the temple was pieced together. A framework of timber scaffolding surrounded the building and supported cranes that hoisted the blocks into position.

Cranes with lifting tongs raised blocks into place

Lifting tongs

Plan of temple

When the column sections, or drums, were in place, stonemasons chiselled the lifting bosses off. Then they carved decorative lines, called flutes, from top to bottom (right).

Timber scaffolding

The temple was built according to a carefully worked-out plan. A master craftsman, called an *architectron*, was in charge of the building work.

Architectron

DAY IN THE LIFE OF A STONEMASON

A stonemason would have got up as early as four o'clock in the morning in the summer months.

Breakfast was bread and fruit with wine to drink, diluted with water. Some bread would be saved for his lunch.

Craftsmen walked to the temple building site, high on the acropolis.

At the building site, all the workers were given their day's instructions by the master craftsman.

Ox-teams pulled wagons from the nearby quarry, bringing more stone blocks to the site.

Stonemasons guided the column drums and stone blocks into place and ensured the lifting ropes were secure.

Methods of attaching blocks to hoists

Metal loops and U-shaped grooves were also used to attach blocks to lifting hoists.

Column sections were not joined using mortar, but with bronze pegs that slotted into holes drilled in the middle of each drum (left).

Types of clamp

Blocks were joined together with iron clamps fitted into slots cut in the stone. Molten lead was poured into the slots to seal them in place.

Slabs around the top of the temple were carved with images in relief (above), which meant they stood out from the surface of the stone.

At midday, when the sun was high in the sky, it was too hot to work. Lunch was eaten in the shade of a tree.

Work continued until around eight o'clock in the evening. In the fading light accidents sometimes happened.

Towards the end of the day the master craftsman might have a meeting to check the temple's progress.

CRAFTSMAN'S TOOLS

1. Iron pincers
2. Iron chisels
3. Wooden mallet
4. Iron drill
5. Angle and plumb-line

THE FINISHED TEMPLE: EXTERIOR

Stonemasons carved detailed images into marble slabs, creating three-dimensional scenes that stood out and were clear to see.

The slabs were lifted into place. Some were fitted at the front of the temple, others became part of the temple's frieze.

The carvings were painted with bright colours. A temple was a colourful building: many look white today because the paint has worn away.

AS A TOWN'S most important religious building, no expense was spared to build and decorate a new temple. It was to become the home for a god or goddess, so only the best was good enough. To use poor quality material or inferior decoration would be a great insult to the deity. A new temple was a status symbol – proof that the town could afford to construct such a glorious building and that it had the skilled stonemasons and decorators to do it. The outside of the finished temple was a splendid sight, a mixture of gleaming marble and richly-painted carvings.

Antefix

At either end of the ridge along the top of the roof was an antefix – a special tile, decorated with a honeysuckle flower design.

Pediment

At each end of the temple was a triangular area called a pediment. It was filled with slabs of stone, carved in relief, usually showing scenes of gods and goddesses from Greek mythology.

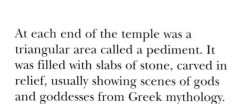

BUILDING TRICKS

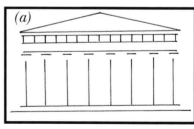

(a)

From the front, temples seem to have perfectly horizontal and vertical lines (a). This was what their builders wanted us to see.

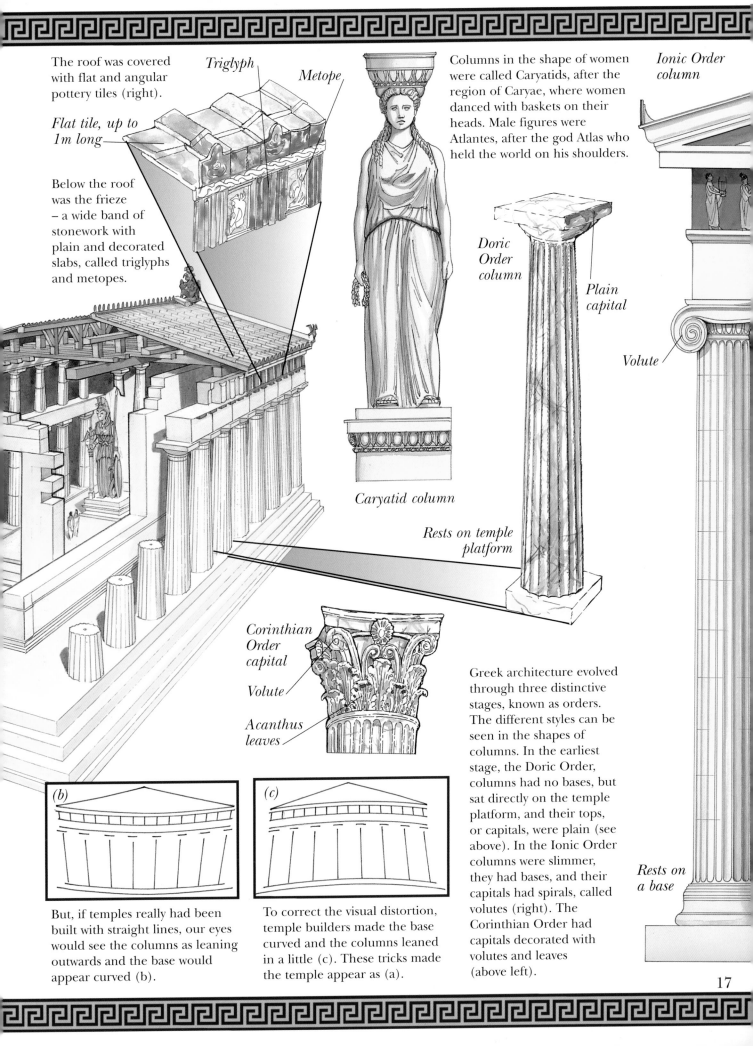

The roof was covered with flat and angular pottery tiles (right).

Flat tile, up to 1m long

Below the roof was the frieze – a wide band of stonework with plain and decorated slabs, called triglyphs and metopes.

Triglyph

Metope

Columns in the shape of women were called Caryatids, after the region of Caryae, where women danced with baskets on their heads. Male figures were Atlantes, after the god Atlas who held the world on his shoulders.

Ionic Order column

Caryatid column

Doric Order column

Plain capital

Volute

Rests on temple platform

Corinthian Order capital

Volute

Acanthus leaves

Greek architecture evolved through three distinctive stages, known as orders. The different styles can be seen in the shapes of columns. In the earliest stage, the Doric Order, columns had no bases, but sat directly on the temple platform, and their tops, or capitals, were plain (see above). In the Ionic Order columns were slimmer, they had bases, and their capitals had spirals, called volutes (right). The Corinthian Order had capitals decorated with volutes and leaves (above left).

Rests on a base

(b)

But, if temples really had been built with straight lines, our eyes would see the columns as leaning outwards and the base would appear curved (b).

(c)

To correct the visual distortion, temple builders made the base curved and the columns leaned in a little (c). These tricks made the temple appear as (a).

17

THE FINISHED TEMPLE: INTERIOR

Molten bronze was poured into clay moulds. When the metal was set, the moulds were broken open.

Ivory, from African elephant tusks, was cut into thin pieces. It was used to form the skin of the statue.

Coloured glass was cast into star-shaped ornaments. They were used to decorate parts of the statue. Each one was like a tiny sparkling jewel.

Gold was beaten into wafer-thin sheets. When applied to the statue's wooden frame, the figure appeared to be made of solid gold.

Underneath its gold and ivory outer surface was the statue's inner frame. It was made entirely from wood.

UNLIKE THE DECORATION OUTSIDE, the inside was relatively plain. It was dark and gloomy because there were no windows. In the main room was a large statue of the town's patron god, who faced the doorway, looking out to the enclosure beyond. The god's spirit was believed to live inside the statue so it was a sacred object and great care was taken in its creation. Greek temples were not used as churches or places of worship, but as a home for a god to live in. When worshippers offered prayers and acts of devotion to the god, they did so in the enclosure around the temple.

Attendants (right) brought offerings of food to the statue even before it was finished – it was their duty to serve and please the god at all times.

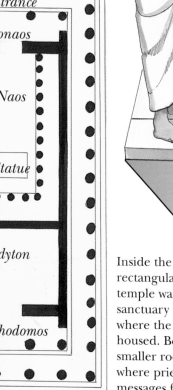

Outer colonnade

Entrance

Pronaos

Naos

Statue

Adyton

Opisthodomos

Attendants

Inside the rectangular temple was the sanctuary (*naos*), where the statue was housed. Behind was a smaller room (*adyton*), where priests delivered messages from the god.

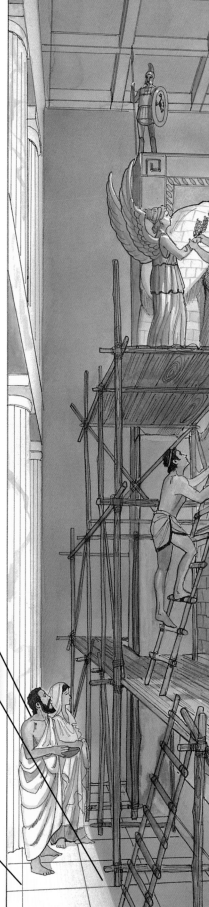

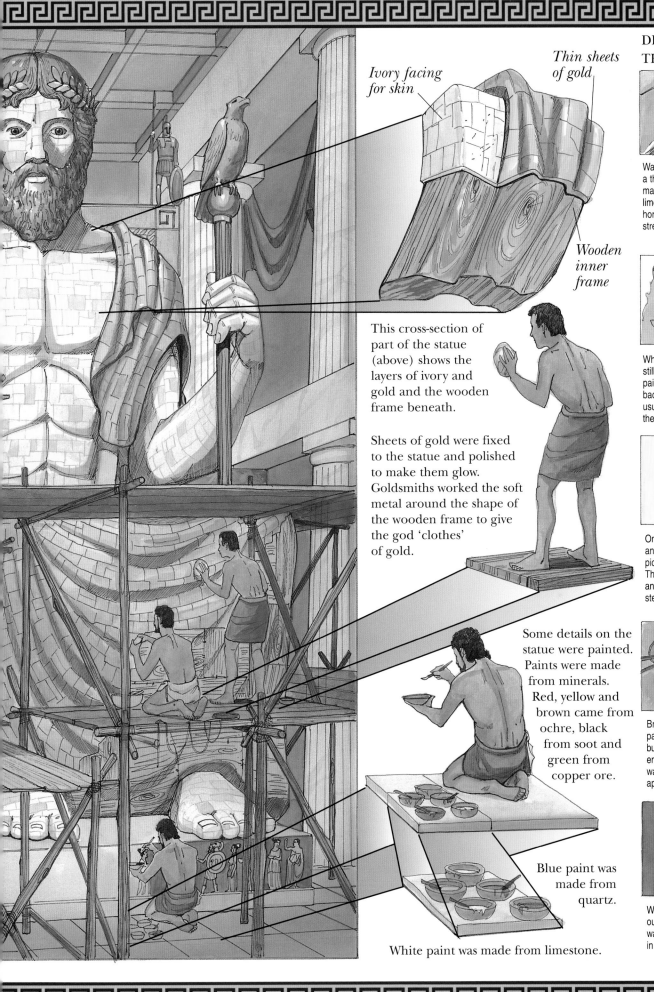

Ivory facing for skin

Thin sheets of gold

Wooden inner frame

This cross-section of part of the statue (above) shows the layers of ivory and gold and the wooden frame beneath.

Sheets of gold were fixed to the statue and polished to make them glow. Goldsmiths worked the soft metal around the shape of the wooden frame to give the god 'clothes' of gold.

Some details on the statue were painted. Paints were made from minerals. Red, yellow and brown came from ochre, black from soot and green from copper ore.

Blue paint was made from quartz.

White paint was made from limestone.

DECORATING THE TEMPLE

Walls were coated with a thin layer of plaster, made from powdered limestone mixed with horsehair to give it strength.

While the plaster was still damp, it was painted all over with a background colour, usually white. It was then left to dry.

On the now white wall, an artist painted a picture in outline only. This was skilled work and required a very steady hand.

Brightly coloured paints were used, but as very little light entered the temple it was not easy to appreciate this.

When the painting's outline was dry, it was carefully filled in with colour.

THE TEMPLE ENCLOSURE

Entrance gateway, or propylon

ALTHOUGH TEMPLES were built to a similar design throughout the Greek world, their sacred enclosures were not. An enclosure could be any size or shape and the layout of the buildings within it followed no set pattern. To enter the enclosure, pilgrims passed through a gateway and, once inside, they were in the spiritual heart of the town. The most important building was the temple where the sacred statue of a god was housed. In front of it, always to the east, was the main altar. Elsewhere were smaller altars, where worshippers could leave gifts and say prayers. The enclosure was a busy place, with people coming and going all day long.

To enter the sacred enclosure, worshippers had to pass through a propylon, or monumental gateway. It was a porch with columns, placed in a side wall of the enclosure. It was put to the side so that on entering the enclosure visitors could marvel at the great size of the temple.

Small altar

Small altar

Sacrificial animal

Main altar

Enclosure wall

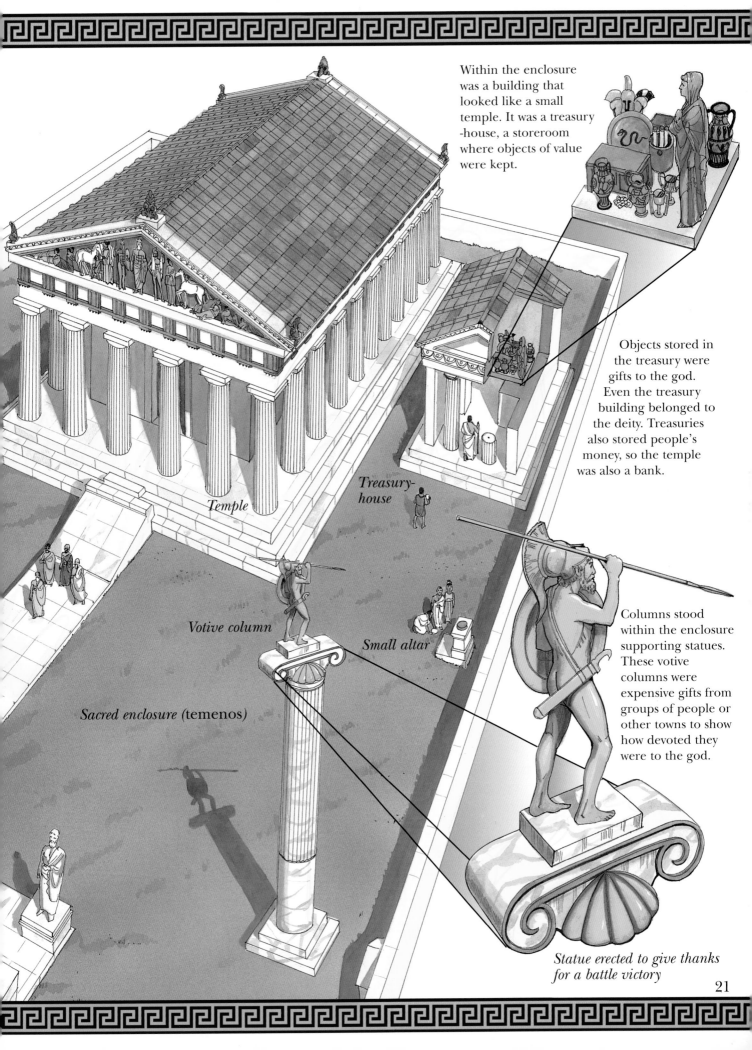

Within the enclosure was a building that looked like a small temple. It was a treasury-house, a storeroom where objects of value were kept.

Objects stored in the treasury were gifts to the god. Even the treasury building belonged to the deity. Treasuries also stored people's money, so the temple was also a bank.

Columns stood within the enclosure supporting statues. These votive columns were expensive gifts from groups of people or other towns to show how devoted they were to the god.

Temple

Treasury-house

Votive column

Small altar

Sacred enclosure (temenos)

Statue erected to give thanks for a battle victory

RELIGION OF THE GREEKS

THE ANCIENT GREEKS believed in many gods and goddesses. The most important were a family of twelve gods called the Olympians, said to live on Mount Olympus, a mountain that seemed to reach up to heaven itself. They were worshipped throughout the Greek world and temples were built in their honour.

There were many lesser gods too, such as Hestia, the goddess of the hearth and home. At one time she had been worshipped as an Olympian, but then her place was taken by Dionysus. The Greeks also believed in and prayed to spirits called nymphs. These shy creatures represented trees, streams and the beauty of nature.

Artemis: goddess of the moon, wild animals, hunting and childbirth. She was protector of all young living creatures and a daughter of Zeus.

Apollo: god of the Sun, truth, music, poetry, dance and healing. The lyre was his symbol and he was a son of Zeus.

Ares: god of war who was cruel and bloodthirsty. He was not a popular god even with his parents, Zeus and Hera.

Dionysus: god of wine, drunkenness, joy and the theatre. The symbol of this son of Zeus was an actor's mask.

Demeter: goddess of grain and fertility and therefore able to nourish humans and animals. She was also Zeus' sister.

Athena: goddess of war, wisdom, art and crafts (such as spinning, weaving, carpentry, metalworking and pottery) and daughter of Zeus.

Demeter

Dionysus

Artemis

Apollo

Ares

Zeus

Hera

Poseidon

Hermes

Aphrodite

Athena

Hephaestus

Zeus: king of the gods. He was god of the weather and a thunderbolt was his symbol. He was both brother and husband of Hera.

Hera: queen of the gods. All Greek women worshipped her as goddess of women, marriage and childbirth. She was Zeus' sister and wife.

Poseidon: god of the sea, earthquakes and horses. The trident, or fish spear, was his symbol and he was Zeus' brother.

Hermes: god of travel, business, weights, measures and sport. This son of Zeus was messenger of the gods who guided souls to the underworld.

Hephaestus: god of fire, volcanoes, blacksmiths and craftsmen. Hera's son, he walked with a limp and was said to be ugly.

Aphrodite: goddess of love and beauty. She had a temper, and was the wife of Hephaestus.

WORSHIPPING THE GODS

THE ANCIENT GREEKS prayed to the gods for guidance and for protection from danger and illness. They gave thanks for prayers the gods appeared to answer. But prayers could be used to bring harm too – hostile prayers, or curses, were sometimes used to bring bad luck.

The Greek gods were believed to be immortal and powerful supreme beings. Humans, on the other hand, were mortal, weak and fragile creatures. Gods and goddesses were treated with great respect and the act of worship was not only a seriously important part of everyday life, it was a duty. Prayers could be said at any time of the day or night. As long as the worshipper provided gifts, the gods would be there for them and would listen.

At the temple at Epidauros, the healer god Asclepius was believed to visit sick people in their dreams. He told them how they could be made well.

They heard stories from the temple priests. One tale told of Asclepius touching a man's hand as he slept. When he awoke, he was cured.

Worshippers were told to leave gifts for Asclepius. Only then would he be able to cure them. Sight could be restored by giving a gift of silver.

Even children who promised gifts for the god had to do as they had said, or Asclepius' healing powers would not work.

Scenes of religious devotion are often found painted on ancient Greek pottery. On this vase (left) a woman is pictured pouring wine into a dish. She is the wife of a warrior and is offering wine to the gods in thanks for the safe return of her husband after a battle.

Altar

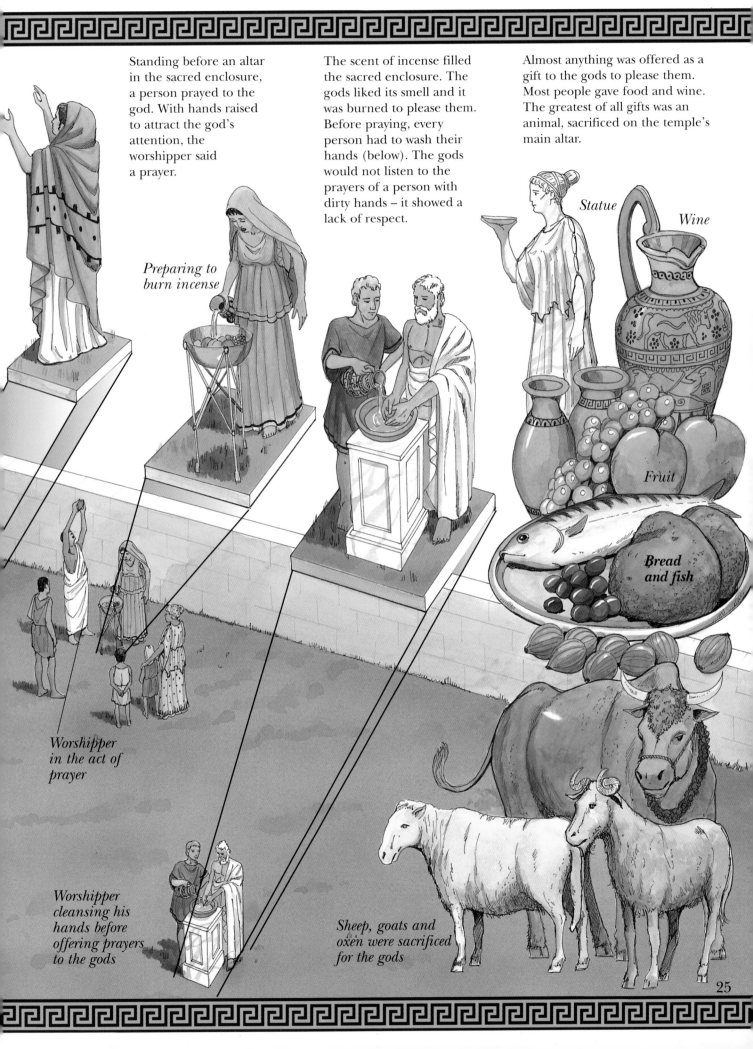

Standing before an altar in the sacred enclosure, a person prayed to the god. With hands raised to attract the god's attention, the worshipper said a prayer.

The scent of incense filled the sacred enclosure. The gods liked its smell and it was burned to please them. Before praying, every person had to wash their hands (below). The gods would not listen to the prayers of a person with dirty hands – it showed a lack of respect.

Almost anything was offered as a gift to the gods to please them. Most people gave food and wine. The greatest of all gifts was an animal, sacrificed on the temple's main altar.

Preparing to burn incense

Statue

Wine

Fruit

Bread and fish

Worshipper in the act of prayer

Worshipper cleansing his hands before offering prayers to the gods

Sheep, goats and oxen were sacrificed for the gods

PREPARING A SACRIFICE

Because sacrificing an animal to the gods was so important, there was a strict procedure to follow. First, prayers were said at the altar.

A small gift of food was offered to the god. Grains of barley were sprinkled on the altar fire to prepare the god to receive the animal offering.

The animal was led to the altar. There were prayers, hymns and music. At the right moment the animal's head was pulled back.

The priest cut the animal's throat with a short, sharp knife. As its blood poured out, its life ebbed away. Soon, it was dead.

GIFTS FOR THE GODS

THERE WAS A GREEK PROVERB which stated, 'Gifts persuade the gods', meaning that if a person gave something to the gods, they would receive something in return. Gifts such as statues, furniture, weapons, clothes and pottery were usually kept in the temple treasury-house, where the gods could make use of them whenever they wished. Food and wine were offered every day at the temple altars and at private shrines in people's homes. Sacrifices were especially important and animals were offered to the gods during rituals within the temple enclosure. Each sacrifice was part of an elaborate ceremony which involved chanting prayers and singing hymns. The ceremony ended with a sacred meal, at which the gods were believed to dine with the worshippers and priests.

The greatest gift to the gods was an ox. The sacred enclosure would be filled with worshippers when such a valuable sacrifice was made.

Ox

Temple attendants supervised the sacrifice ceremony, ensuring the ritual was carried out correctly.

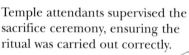

Temple attendant

The dead animal was cut into pieces. Its leg bones were removed and wrapped in fat as the gifts to the gods.

While the fat-covered leg bones burned away on the altar fire, the rest of the meat was carefully roasted.

Worshippers and priests ate the roasted meat, which was believed to be filled with the god's power. Wine was poured over the meat and then into cups. As they drank, worshippers felt they were drinking with the god.

Priest

Sacrificial animal

Jar filled with wine

Bowl for washing in

Aulos

A priest led a procession to the main altar in the enclosure. On his tray were the items he would need for the sacrifice: a knife, wine and barley.

As the procession moved towards the altar, musicians played instruments, such as the _aulos_, which was like a double flute. String instruments, called lyres, were plucked and cymbals were struck. Priests and worshippers chanted the sacred words of the sacrifice service.

A scene from a piece of painted pottery (left) shows a pig being sacrificed to the gods. In Athens, a pig was sacrificed before every meeting of the city's Assembly.

THE PRIESTHOOD

A priest was given a share of the meat from a sacrificed animal and also its hide.

Most priests received free housing. They lived in buildings inside the temple's sacred enclosure, or in houses in the town.

Some priests were paid a salary. The amount they received depended on how rich their god's cult was and how many people visited the temple.

At some temples, priests were given crowns made from golden laurel leaves. Each crown was worth 1,000 drachmas – a huge sum of money.

Even after a priest had left the priesthood he was still rewarded for his service, claiming free meals for example.

IN ANCIENT GREEK SOCIETY, a person was usually born into the priesthood. A child from a priestly family knew that one day they would become a priest or priestess. Only the request of a dying priest would allow someone outside the family to replace him. Priests were important people in the community. They were believed to have the power to talk to the gods and so were respected and trusted. Because people believed the gods controlled all aspects of daily life, they called on their priests whenever they needed help.

Incense

Priests were usually adults, but at a temple in Rhodes, there were boy priests.

Boy priest

Female priestess

Male priest

A priest also had the right to erect a statue of himself. It reminded people that he had seen to their spiritual needs.

A priest who had given special service might also have been rewarded with the best seats at the theatre, on the front row.

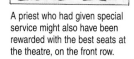

After the birth of a baby, a priest visited the house where it had been born (above). He offered prayers to the gods, giving thanks for the creation of a new life. He burned sweet-smelling incense to purify the house and to bring the gods' blessing to the home and those who lived there.

Most members of the priesthood were men, but there were women priestesses. Usually, priests served gods and priestesses served goddesses. At some temples both male and female gods were worshipped, so priests and priestesses worked alongside each other.

Mourners

Witnesses   Bridegroom   Bride   Priest

Priests conducted marriage ceremonies. They were held in the home of the bride's father, in the presence of witnesses, but the bride herself did not have to be present. A few days after the ceremony there was a feast, with plenty of singing and music.

It was a priest's duty to serve the temple and its god. He made sure the temple was run properly. This involved a lot of administration work.

Only members of the priesthood could directly communicate with the gods. When people wanted to contact them, they asked a priest to act as the go-between and he offered their gifts to the gods (right).

If a worshipper behaved badly, or did something that might offend the god, a priest could order him to pay a fine.

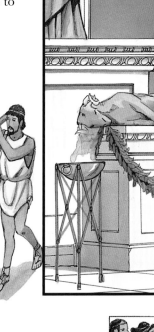

Priests were in charge of the temple treasury-house, where gifts to the gods were stored.

Some visitors to temples had travelled long distances and it was the priest's job to offer them hospitality.

At a funeral (left), a priest led the procession of mourners to the cemetery. Prayers were said, women wailed and musicians played.

The dead person was carried head first

It was every priest's duty to serve the spiritual needs of the people, from birth to death.

Priests organized the temple's festivals and sacrifices according to the exact rules and rituals.

Priests were in charge of building and repair work for their temple.

FESTIVALS

FESTIVALS were an important part of the religious and social life of a town. They were held throughout the year, to praise and honour the gods and every town had its own calendar of festivals. The weeks were not divided into working days and rest days, so festivals provided a welcome relief from daily work.

In Athens, seven days of every month were devoted to festivals. All normal work stopped and people relaxed, it was a time for families to be together. Most people lived on an everyday diet of bread, vegetables, dairy products, fish and fruit, but festivals provided feasts of meat from sacrificial animals.

Because meat was expensive, oxen were only sacrificed at major festivals. Sheep and pigs were the usual sacrificial animals.

Temple

Most festivals included a procession to the temple of the town's god (right). Priests led the way, chanting prayers so that they sounded half sung, half spoken. The prayers were well-known and people joined in. As the procession slowly made its way to the acropolis, it stopped several times for hymns to be sung. Animals for sacrifice were also part of the procession. Once everyone had passed through the entrance gateway and into the sacred enclosure, the service of sacrifice began.

THE FARMING YEAR

Most festivals were linked to the farming year, and were held to bless the fields and crops. Farmers were the most respected of all Greek workers because they provided food for the population, but food was only provided if the gods willed it.

The farming year began in February. Fields were ploughed, the soil was cleared of stones, and barley seeds were planted.

In March, vineyards were attended to. The grapevines were tidied up and new shoots were trained along string.

Sheep were sheared in April. Their fleeces were washed, then spun into wool for clothes and blankets.

Also in April, farmers cut grass in their fields. When it was dry, it was gathered up and stored for animal feed for the winter.

Music was an essential part of religious life. In fact, music was thought of as a gift from the gods to humankind. The gods were said to have invented some of the instruments played by earthly musicians.

Singer and musicians

Aulos

Tambourine

Syrinx

Kithara

Entrance gateway

Greek musicians played a variety of wind, string and percussion instruments, including the tambourine, the *aulos* and the *syrinx*. The *kithara* was a small harp with strings to be plucked.

Some festivals were for men only and some were just for women. Others were open to everyone, citizens and non-citizens, including slaves.

By May the barley crop was ripening and it was time for the harvest. It was cut by hand using iron sickles.

In a good year the harvest continued throughout June and July. Donkeys carried baskets of grain to the town's grain stores.

The grape harvest began in July. The black and green grapes from the vines were fermented to make wine.

In July, olives were collected. The branches of olive trees were beaten and the ripe fruit fell into sheets spread on the ground.

Wheat was harvested in August. As it was tossed into the air, the wind blew the unwanted husks away, leaving the grains.

Cheese was made in September and October. It was usually made from goats' milk.

Fortune-tellers observed the flight and calls of birds, from which they claimed to be able to predict the future.

Examining the liver of a sacrificed animal was another method of fortune-telling. A healthy liver was a good omen, a diseased liver was a bad sign.

Some fortune-tellers said they could see into a person's future by interpreting their dreams. This was taken very seriously.

If a person sneezed, it was considered to be a sign from the gods that something bad was going to happen to them.

If a person whispered to a god's temple statue, they listened for a reply in the conversations of strangers.

ORACLES, OMENS AND FORTUNE-TELLERS

Attendant to translate the oracle's strange words

THE ANCIENT GREEKS were superstitious people who believed in miracles and magic. They told stories about heroes who came back from the dead and gods who had mysterious powers. They believed that 'little demons' (*keres*) were forever trying to harm them by bringing illness and bad luck. They asked fortune-tellers to predict the future and consulted oracles – people who were believed to be the gods' messengers on Earth. There were omens everywhere. By learning how to read these 'signals from the gods', people were able to prepare themselves for what the future might bring.

The temple's god communicates through the oracle

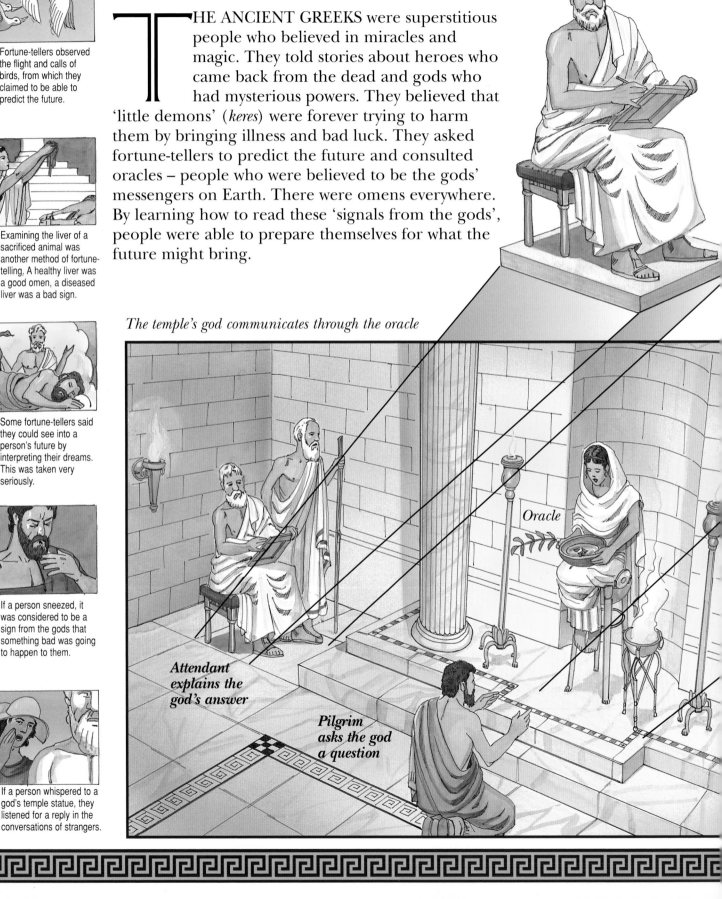

Oracle

Attendant explains the god's answer

Pilgrim asks the god a question

At the Temple of Apollo at Delphi, there was a wise oracle priestess (right). After chewing *laurus nobilis* (bay leaves), she fell into a trance, then spoke strange words in answer to a pilgrim's question.

Oracle priestess

Fumes from burning bay leaves

Picture from an ancient Greek vase showing that even kings consulted oracles

The oracle's words were thought to be messages from the god. A male attendant (left) was able to understand them and it was his job to explain their meaning to pilgrims.

Burning bay leaves (above) gave off a strong vapour, which the priestess inhaled. The fumes affected her mind and in this trance-like state the god could talk through her.

The god Apollo was said to have slain a dragon at Delphi whose dead body gave off a gas. The temple was built over the hole in the ground where the gas came from and the temple priestess breathed this in along with the bayleaf fumes.

Temple of Apollo at Delphi

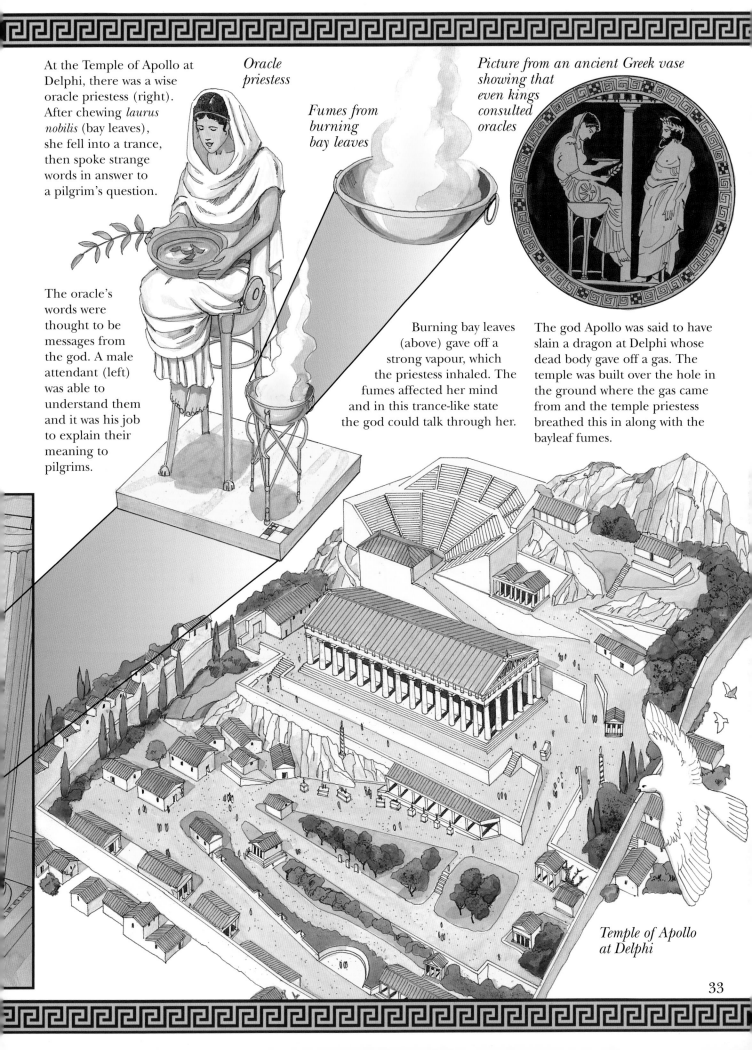

Temples of the Ancient Greek World

FOR 200 YEARS, starting in the 8th century BC, Greek settlers sailed to other lands and built new towns around the coast of the Mediterranean Sea and Black Sea. Wherever the Greeks settled they took their culture and society with them. These new Greek colonies each had a 'mother' town, called a *metropolis*, back home in Greece – the town where the Greek settlers had originally come from. The laws, customs and religious cults of the metropolis were adopted by the colony. Temples were built in colonies throughout the Greek world, following the same orders, or styles, of architecture used in Greece itself.

TEMPLE OF ZEUS
Olympia, Greece, c.460 BC
Built in the Doric style from limestone faced with marble, inside was a 12-m tall gold and ivory statue of Zeus which was famous as one of the Seven Wonders of the Ancient World.

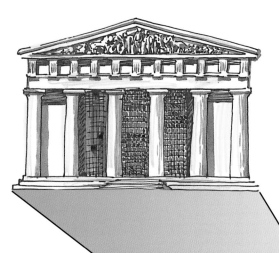

TEMPLE OF POSEIDON
Paestum, Italy, c.460 BC
One of the most perfectly preserved Greek temples, built in the Doric style at the Greek city of Poseidonia. The Romans renamed the city Paestum.

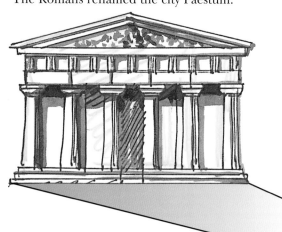

TEMPLE OF ZEUS OLYMPIUS
Agrigentum, Sicily, c.500 BC
The largest of all known Greek temples, built in the Doric style, with a floor plan larger than a football pitch. Twice the height of the Parthenon at Athens, its roof was held up by Atlantes – male statues each 7.6 m tall.

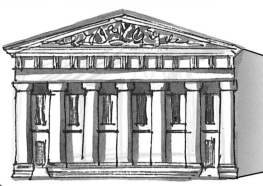

ITALY

Neapolis

Poseidonia (Paestum)

Sybaris

Kroton

So many Greek colonies were established in southern Italy and Sicily that the area became known as *Magna Graecia*, meaning 'Greater Greece'.

Himera

Rhegion

SICILY • *Naxos*

Akragas (Agrigentum) • *Syracuse*

MEDITERRANEAN SEA

TEMPLE OF APHAIA (below)
Aegina, Greece, c.490 BC
A Doric-style temple on an
island, a short distance from
Athens. Made from limestone
faced with white marble, it was
richly decorated with many
painted sculptures.

TEMPLE OF APOLLO (left)
Corinth, Greece, c.540 BC
One of the first major temples
built in the Doric style. It stood
in the marketplace (*agora*) of
Corinth, rather than on the
town's acropolis.

THE PARTHENON (below)
Athens, Greece, 447-432 BC
(see page 36)

GREECE

Athens

Olympia *Aegina*
Corinth
Aegina

IONIA

Samos
Ephesus

AEGEAN SEA

CRETE

TEMPLE OF ARTEMIS
Ephesus, Turkey, c.360 BC
One of the Seven Wonders of the Ancient
World, this huge, highly decorated temple was
built in the Ionic style at a Greek city in Ionia
(a region along the west coast of modern-day
Turkey). The temple had 117 columns, each
18 m tall. Many of the columns were carved
with relief sculptures around their bases.

THE PARTHENON

LIKE OTHER GREEK CITIES, Athens had an acropolis, where the city built its temples. The greatest of these has become known as the Parthenon. In 449 BC, the war between the Athenians and Persians ended. In celebration of the peace, Pericles, the leading Athenian statesman, set about turning Athens into a city of beauty. In just 15 years the Acropolis was transformed, as a new temple was built in honour of the city's patron goddess, Athena Parthenos. Inside the marble temple stood her magnificent statue, smothered from head to toe in gold. Outside, the building was adorned with some of the finest sculptures ever to be placed on a temple. The Parthenon became a symbol of the great city of Athens.

The temple was 69.5 m long and 30.9 m wide

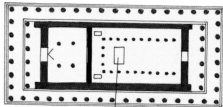

Statue of Athena

A plan of the Parthenon reveals its long, narrow shape. The sacred statue of Athena was placed in the very centre of the temple, facing the doorway at the east end.

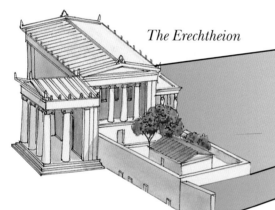

The Erechtheion

The Erechtheion temple was named after King Erechtheus, the legendary first king of Athens. It was built soon after the Parthenon, on the site where it was said Athena had placed the first olive tree in Athens.

Statue of Athena

As worshippers walked through the sacred enclosure towards the Parthenon they passed a huge bronze statue of Athena. Pilgrims offered prayers to the goddess before moving on to her temple home.

PLANNING THE PARTHENON

In the early 440s BC, Athens rose to a position of power over other Greek cities. They paid taxes to Athens and the city grew rich. The money was used to build the Parthenon.

Plans for the new building were drawn up by master craftsmen.

Perhaps a small-scale model of the temple was built, before the real work began.

Regular meetings were held at which the temple's progress was discussed.

Sculptors came from all over Greece to work on the temple's statues and decorations.

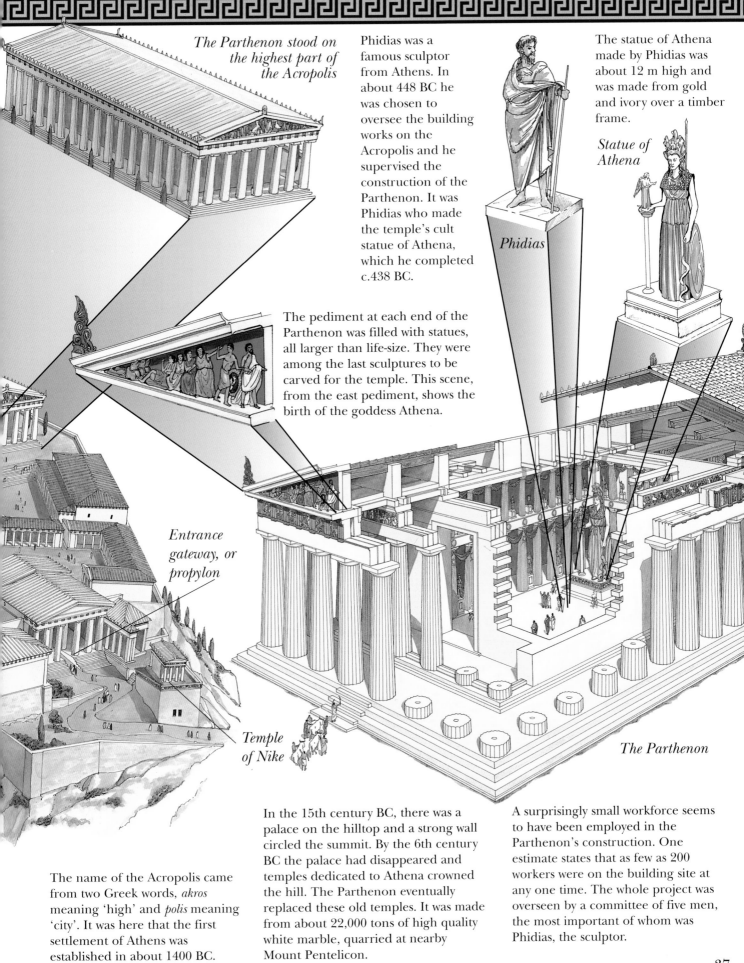

The Parthenon stood on the highest part of the Acropolis

Phidias was a famous sculptor from Athens. In about 448 BC he was chosen to oversee the building works on the Acropolis and he supervised the construction of the Parthenon. It was Phidias who made the temple's cult statue of Athena, which he completed c.438 BC.

The statue of Athena made by Phidias was about 12 m high and was made from gold and ivory over a timber frame.

Statue of Athena

Phidias

The pediment at each end of the Parthenon was filled with statues, all larger than life-size. They were among the last sculptures to be carved for the temple. This scene, from the east pediment, shows the birth of the goddess Athena.

Entrance gateway, or propylon

Temple of Nike

The Parthenon

The name of the Acropolis came from two Greek words, *akros* meaning 'high' and *polis* meaning 'city'. It was here that the first settlement of Athens was established in about 1400 BC.

In the 15th century BC, there was a palace on the hilltop and a strong wall circled the summit. By the 6th century BC the palace had disappeared and temples dedicated to Athena crowned the hill. The Parthenon eventually replaced these old temples. It was made from about 22,000 tons of high quality white marble, quarried at nearby Mount Pentelicon.

A surprisingly small workforce seems to have been employed in the Parthenon's construction. One estimate states that as few as 200 workers were on the building site at any one time. The whole project was overseen by a committee of five men, the most important of whom was Phidias, the sculptor.

THE PANATHENAEA FESTIVAL

THE GREATEST FESTIVAL in Athens was the Panathenaea, meaning 'all Athenian'. It was held on the 28th day of the month of Hecatombaion (July and August in our calendar) in honour of the birth of Athena, the city's patron deity. Every fourth year, the Great Panathenaea was held, combining 12 days of sport, poetry and music competitions with a procession that made its way through the city to the Acropolis. At the head of the procession were the priestesses of Athena, followed by women with gifts. Behind them were the sacrificial animals (100 cows and some sheep), musicians and a ship dragged on wheels. From its mast hung a huge *peplos*, or robe – a gift from the people of Athens to their goddess. Inside the Parthenon the peplos was given to Athena's statue, where it stayed for the next four years. The animals were sacrificed and their meat was eaten.

THE PARTHENON FRIEZE

Below the roof of the Parthenon and running around all four sides of the *naos* was a decorated frieze carved from marble.

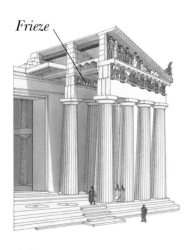

Frieze

The sculpted panels of the Parthenon frieze can be read like a picture strip. The theme is the procession of the Panathenaea festival. It begins at the back (west end) of the temple and runs along both sides to meet at the front (east end). The sculptors went to great trouble to carve the reliefs in fine detail, showing, (a) sacrificial animals, (b) tray-bearers, (c) musicians, (d) elders, (e) charioteers and (f) horsemen. The most important carvings were placed along the front of the temple, showing (g) the maidens who wove Athena's peplos, (h, i) gods and, in the centre, a young girl handing Athena's sacred peplos to a senior priest of the temple (j). The frieze was painted in bright colours and some of the figures had bronze sandals and armour fitted to them.

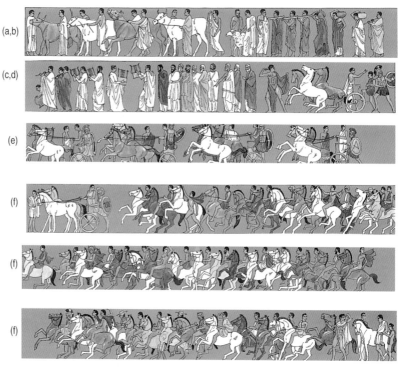

(a,b)

(c,d)

(e)

(f)

(f)

(f)

(d,e)

(a,f)

(f)

(g)

(h)

(j)

(i)

The statue of Athena was covered in more than 100 kg of gold

Nike, winged goddess of victory

Athena's giant peplos was made by the weavers of Athens. No one knows how it was displayed inside the temple. Perhaps it was hung from the ceiling or draped over the statue's shoulders.

THE PARTHENON IN HISTORY

THE CITIZENS OF ATHENS must have thought their world would last for ever. But to the west of Greece a new power was emerging in Italy and, in 146 BC, Greece was conquered by the Romans. They adopted much of the Greek culture, including the Greek gods and goddesses, to whom they gave Roman names. The Greek goddess Athena became the Roman goddess Minerva. Worship continued at the Parthenon, but when Rome adopted Christianity, the temple was converted into a church. This happened in the 5th century AD, by which time the Parthenon was almost 1,000 years old.

In 1458, Athens was conquered by Moslem Turks, who turned the Parthenon into a mosque. In 1687, a Venetian army, from Italy, besieged the Turks and it was then that the 2,130-year-old Parthenon was blown up. In the early 1800s, an English nobleman, along with several other Europeans, removed many of the Parthenon's statues and relief sculptures. Today, the temple is slowly being restored to its former glory.

Church *Bell-tower*

When the Parthenon became a church in the medieval period (above), windows were cut in its walls to let light in and the statues of the pagan gods were defaced.

When it became a mosque (below), a minaret was added to the bell-tower, from where the faithful were called to prayer.

Minaret

On 26 September, 1687, a cannonball from a Venetian cannon landed on the Parthenon (right). Barrels of gunpowder stored inside the building exploded and the Parthenon was destroyed.

Roman visitors to Athens worshipped in the Parthenon and bought souvenirs from the city's markets, such as models of the statue of Athena.

After the explosion in the 17th century, the Parthenon lay in ruins. The frieze had been brought down and columns were toppled. The Turks cleared the centre of the building and built a new mosque there in 1776, using pieces of fallen masonry. Other pieces were taken from the Acropolis to build new buildings in Athens. Some stones were even burned to make lime, from which building mortar was made.

A lucky shot from a cannon destroyed the Parthenon

Earl of Elgin

In 1801, the Earl of Elgin (1766-1841), the British diplomat to the Turkish rulers of Athens, was given permission by them to remove sculptures from the Parthenon (right).

In 1816, Lord Elgin's collection from the Parthenon was bought by the British Museum for £35,000.

Today, visitors travel from all over the world to see the Parthenon. The temple is being restored and a new museum is being built.

TIMESPAN

40,000-6500 BC The first inhabitants of Greece were groups of prehistoric hunter-gatherers. They lived during the Palaeolithic (Old Stone Age) and Mesolithic (Middle Stone Age) periods. This was a time before humankind had learned how to make objects from metal. These early communities lived in temporary campsites, often inside caves and rock shelters. This is where archaeologists have found evidence of them, such as hand axes and scrapers made from stone. Bones from ibex, chamois, deer, beaver, wolf and badger tell us about the animals they hunted.

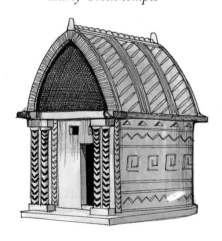

Early Greek temple

6500-3200 BC The nomadic lifestyle of the hunter-gatherers gradually disappeared as people settled down in one place. A new period of human history began, called the Neolithic (New Stone Age). Agriculture became an important way of life – for the first time, people began to farm the land, growing cereal crops such as wheat and barley. Animals were tamed, providing a source of meat and milk. The first villages were built and the first pottery was made. But it was still a prehistoric era, a time before writing.

Statue of the goddess Athena

3200-1100 BC Metal was used for the first time in the Bronze Age period and the first civilizations appeared. On Crete and other islands in the Aegean Sea, people built towns and huge palaces with many rooms. This Minoan civilization was named after King Minos, who was said to have lived on Crete at that time. Meanwhile, the first Greek-speaking people settled in mainland Greece. These were the Mycenaeans, named after the citadel of Mycenae. They lived in hilltop towns surrounded by strong walls. Writing was used by both the Minoans and the Mycenaeans – the written history of Greece had begun.

A Minoan bull-leaping ceremony

1100-800 BC The Minoan and Mycenaean civilizations both ended at about the same time and Greece entered a time of unrest and hardship. During this Dark Age, iron was introduced to Greece from the east. It was far harder than bronze and was used for tools and weapons. For a time, people forgot how to write – which is how this period got its name: society appeared to stop developing.

800-500 BC As the Dark Age ended, Greece entered a period of recovery. This was the Archaic Age, when Greek society began to develop into what would be a great civilization in the centuries that followed. The population increased and cities such as Athens, Olympia, Corinth and Sparta became major centres.

As they gained control of their surrounding land they became city-states. Greece became a patchwork of such city-states – powerful self-governing cities that often competed against each other. The Archaic Age was also the time of greatest expansion overseas, when many new Greek colonies were established around the coastlines of the Mediterranean Sea and Black Sea. The first major festivals were held during this period too, such as the Olympic Games, which began in 776 BC. The Greek alphabet was invented (c.775 BC) and the art of writing returned (c.750 BC), after a 200-year period during which nothing had been written at all.

A Caryatid column

The economy developed and the first Greek coins were minted (c.590 BC). In c.505 BC a new style of government was introduced in Athens called 'democracy', meaning 'power by the people'. Ordinary citizens were given the power to make decisions about how their city should be governed.

Gifts for the gods

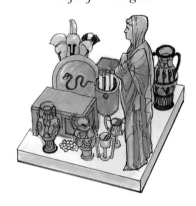

500-323 BC This Classical Period or 'golden age' was marked by the blossoming of Greek culture. The best Greek poets, playwrights, historians, philosophers, doctors, public speakers, astronomers, mathematicians, scientists and statesmen lived and worked during this time. Towns made themselves beautiful with the construction of grand buildings, such as the Parthenon in Athens. But it was also a time of conflict, when wars were fought between the Greeks and the Persians, the traditional enemies of Greece. There was also a war between the Greek city-states of Athens and Sparta,

which ended in victory for Sparta in 404 BC. The final years of the Classical Period saw the conquests of Alexander the Great, who battled to gain a vast empire for Greece stretching as far as India.

323-30 BC Alexander the Great died in 323 BC and his empire split into separate kingdoms, each with its own capital. They were called Hellenistic kingdoms, from the Greek word *hellazein* meaning 'to speak Greek or identify with the Greeks'. People in these lands continued to have a Greek way of life. While Alexander's empire was breaking apart, a new one was spreading from the west – the Roman Empire. In 146 BC mainland Greece became a province of the Roman Empire and when Egypt, the last of the Hellenistic kingdoms, came under Roman rule in 30 BC, the domination of the ancient Greek civilization came to an end.

Ancient Greek musical instruments

Glossary

Acropolis (ak-rop-o-liss) The hill which formed the religious centre of most Greek towns.

Adyton (ad-i-ton) Inner, private room of a temple, usually behind the *naos*.

Agora Open space used for holding a town market and doing business.

Altar Flat-topped block used to make offerings to a god.

Antefix A decorative roof tile.

Architectron (ark-e-tek-tron) The master craftsman in charge of a building project.

Assembly The gathering of the citizens of a Greek town and the land it governs.

Aulos (or loss) Wind instrument, like a flute.

Boss A protruding piece of stone on a block to which lifting ropes were attached.

Bouleuterion (boo-lu-teer-ee-on) Council house where a town's officials met.

Capital The decorated top of a column.

Caryatid (ka-ree-at-id) A statue of a woman, used like a column.

Citadel A fortified place.

Colonnade A series of columns in a straight line that support a roof.

Council A town's elected officials.

Cult The worship of a particular deity.

Deity A supernatural being worshipped by people, such as a god or goddess.

Flutes Vertical grooves that run up and down a building's columns.

Frieze A continuous pattern of decoration.

Immortal Able to live forever. Gods and goddesses were immortal.

Incense Sweet-smelling vapour made by burning gums and spices.

Keres (ke-reez) Little demons that the ancient Greeks believed tormented and troubled people.

Kithara (ki-tha-ra) A musical instrument with strings; like a small harp.

Lyre A musical instrument with strings – smaller than a *kithara*.

Magna Graecia (mag-na gray-ke-a) The parts of southern Italy and Sicily where Greek colonies were established, meaning 'Greater Greece'.

Marmaros The Greek word for marble, a hard, shiny stone.

Metope A carved stone slab that formed part of a frieze.

Metropolis A 'mother town' in Greece to which overseas Greek colonies belonged.

Naos (nay-oss) The innermost part of a Greek temple where the cult statue of the god or goddess was kept.

Ochre A natural pigment (colour) used to make paint.

Olympians The twelve most important gods and goddesses.

Omen A sign, said to be from the gods, which warned of good or evil to come.

Opisthodomos (op-iss-tho-doe-muss) Rear porch of a temple.

Oracle The sacred place where pilgrims went to consult a deity; the priest or priestess who the deity spoke through; the message from the deity.

Order A style of architecture that has certain characteristics.

Ostracism (oss-tra-siz-um) Process of sending a person into exile.

Panathenaea (pan-ath-en-ay-a) The main religious festival in Athens.

Patron In religion, a deity regarded as a protector.

Pediment The triangular area below the roof at each end of a building.

Peplos A garment worn by Greek women.

Poros The Greek word for limestone, a soft type of stone.

Pronaos (pro-nay-oss) The front porch of a Greek temple.

Propylon (prop-ee-lon) Monumental entrance gateway leading to a temple's sacred enclosure.

Relief Carvings which stand out from a background.

Syrinx (sir-inx) A woodwind musical instrument, also known as the Pipes of Pan.

Temenos (tem-en-oss) Sacred enclosure in which a temple stands.

Treasury-house Storeroom where gifts to the gods were housed.

Triglyph (trig-liff) A plain stone slab that formed part of a frieze.

Volute Scroll-like decoration seen on some column capitals.

INDEX Page numbers in bold refer to illustrations

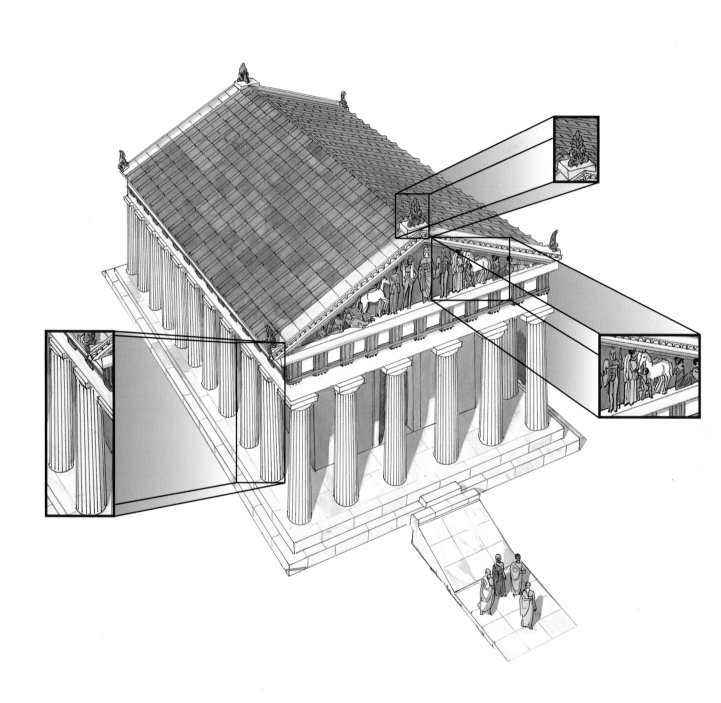